PIANO/VOCAL/GUITAR

· THE BEST OF ·
COLE PORTER

CONTENTS

ISBN 0-7935-1517-3

HAL•LEONARD®
CORPORATION
7777 W. BLUEMOUND RD. P.O. BOX 13819 MILWAUKEE, WI 53213

ALL OF YOU

Words and Music by
COLE PORTER

ALLEZ-VOUS-EN, GO AWAY

Words and Music by
COLE PORTER

blind when I view the blue of your eyes.

poco rit

There-fore, please do not take me to task

a tempo

if the fol - low - ing fa - vor I ask:

rit

Refrain *(Slow Valse tempo with much expression)*

Al - lez-vous - en,* al - lez-vous - en, {Mam' - selle, {M' - sieur,

legato

p

*Pronounce: Al-lay-voo-zon
(French for Go away.)

ANYTHING GOES

Words and Music by
COLE PORTER

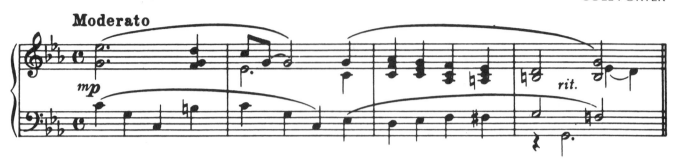

VERSE

Times have changed____ And we've of-ten re-

wound the clock____ Since the Pu-ri-tans got a shock____

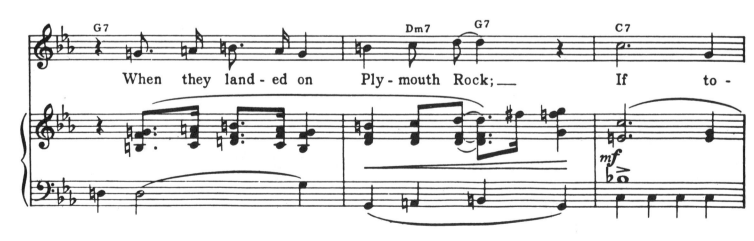

When they land-ed on Ply-mouth Rock;____ If to-

REFRAIN

AT LONG LAST LOVE

Words and Music by
COLE PORTER

17

ANOTHER OP'NIN', ANOTHER SHOW

(From "KISS ME KATE")

Words and Music by
COLE PORTER

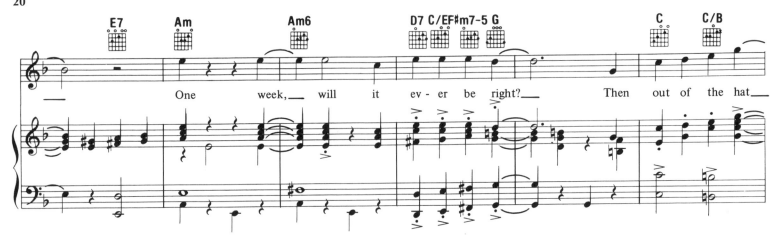

One week,___ will it ev-er be right?___ Then out of the hat___

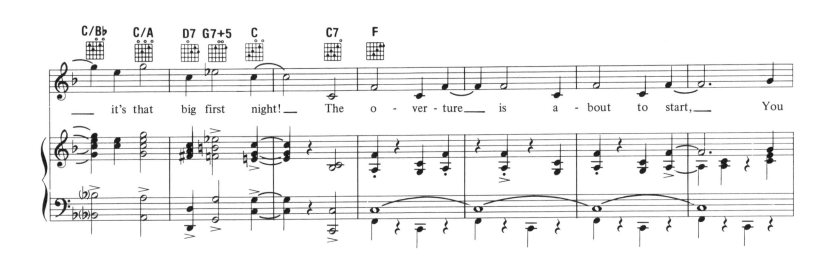

___ it's that big first night! The o-ver-ture___ is a-bout to start,___ You

cross your fin-gers and hold your heart,___ It's cur-tain time___ and a-

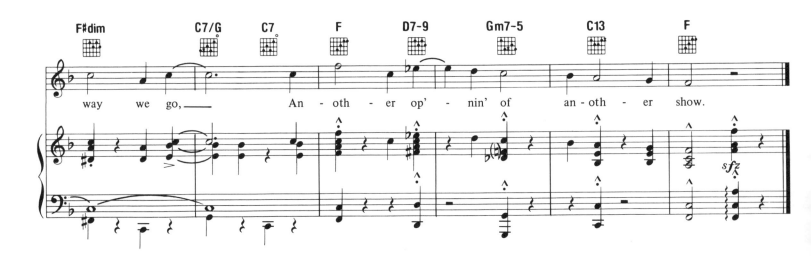

way we go,___ An-oth-er op'-nin' of an-oth-er show.

BLOW, GABRIEL, BLOW

Words and Music by
COLE PORTER

REFRAIN

24

BE A CLOWN

Words and Music by
COLE PORTER

BEGIN THE BEGUINE

Words and Music by
COLE PORTER

BRUSH UP YOUR SHAKESPEARE
(From "KISS ME KATE")

Words and Music by
COLE PORTER

39

* *Cockney for take*

EASY TO LOVE

(From "BORN TO DANCE")

Words and Music by
COLE PORTER

I know too well that I'm _____ just wast-ing pre - cious time in

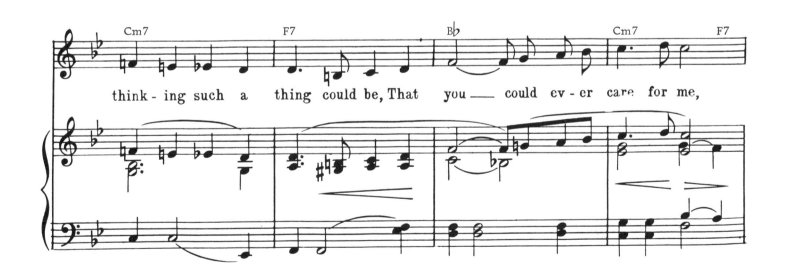

think - ing such a thing could be, That you _____ could ev - er care for me,

42

C'EST MAGNIFIQUE

Words and Music by
COLE PORTER

soon you will find, if you fol-low your heart, not your mind,

Love is wait-ing there a-gain, to take you up in the

air a - gain.

Refrain (*Slow and easy*)

When love comes in and takes you for a

46

spin, oo la la-la,_____ *C'est mag - ni -

fi - que. When ev - 'ry night your

loved one holds you tight, oo la la-la,___ C'est mag - ni -

fi - que. But when, one day, your

*Pronounced "say man-yee-fee-kuh"

DON'T FENCE ME IN

Words and Music by
COLE PORTER

FRIENDSHIP

Words and Music by
COLE PORTER

FROM THIS MOMENT ON

Words and Music by
COLE PORTER

I CONCENTRATE ON YOU
(From "BROADWAY MELODY OF 1940")

Words and Music by
COLE PORTER

63

GET OUT OF TOWN

Words and Music by
COLE PORTER

The farce was end_ed, The cur-tains drawn,

And I at least pre-tend-ed That love was dead and gone.

I GET A KICK OUT OF YOU

Words and Music by
COLE PORTER

I LOVE PARIS

Words and Music by
COLE PORTER

73

I LOVE YOU

Words and Music by
COLE PORTER

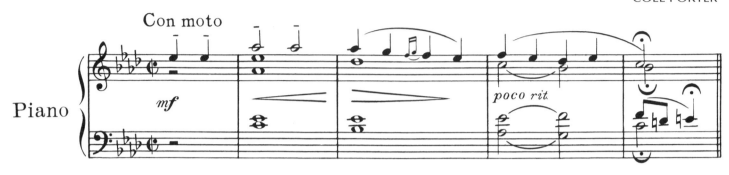

If a love song I could on-ly write,___ A song with words and

mu-sic di-vine ___ I would ser - e - nade you ev-'ry

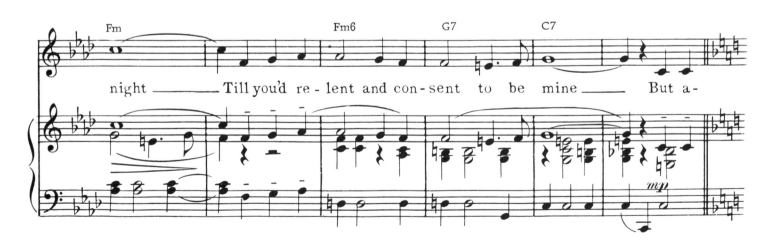

night ___ Till you'd re-lent and con-sent to be mine ___ But a-

78

80

IN THE STILL OF THE NIGHT

Words and Music by
COLE PORTER

I'VE GOT YOU UNDER MY SKIN

Words and Music by
COLE PORTER

IT'S ALL RIGHT WITH ME

Words and Music by
COLE PORTER

IT'S DE-LOVELY

Words and Music by
COLE PORTER

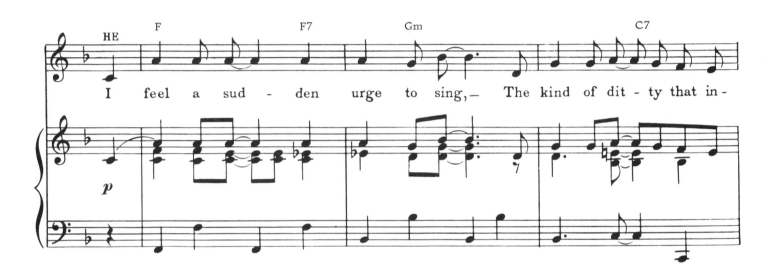

I feel a sud - den urge to sing,— The kind of dit - ty that in-

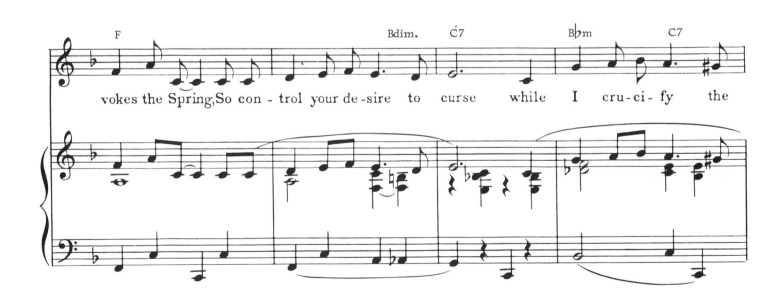

vokes the Spring, So con - trol your de - sire to curse while I cru - ci - fy the

96

* *Pronounced "delukes".*

JUST ONE OF THOSE THINGS

Words and Music by
COLE PORTER

103

LET'S DO IT
(LET'S FALL IN LOVE)

Words and Music by
COLE PORTER

SO IN LOVE
(From "KISS ME KATE")

Words and Music by
COLE PORTER

Moderately

Strange, dear,_____ but true, dear,_____ When I'm close_____ to you, dear,_____ The stars fill the sky,_____ So in love with you am I,_____

LOVE FOR SALE

Words and Music by
COLE PORTER

Who would like to sam-ple my sup - ply? _____ Who's pre-pared to

pay the price For a trip to par-a-dise? Love _____ for sale. _____

Let the po - ets pipe of love In their child-ish way,

I know ev - 'ry type of love Bet-ter far than, they. If you want the

thrill of love, I've been thru the mill of love; Old love, new love,

MY HEART BELONGS TO DADDY

(From "LEAVE IT TO ME")

Words and Music by
COLE PORTER

heart be-longs_ to Dad-dy, Da-da, da-da-da, da-da-da - ad! So I

want to warn_ you, lad-die, Tho' I know you're per - fect - ly

swell, That my heart be-longs_ to Dad-dy __ 'Cause my

Dad-dy, he treats it so well. While well. ___

NIGHT AND DAY

Words and Music by
COLE PORTER

Like the beat, beat, beat, of the tom-tom; When the jun - gle shad - ows fall, Like the tick, tick, tock of the state - ly clock, as it stands a - gainst the wall, Like the drip, drip, drip, of the rain-drops, When the sum - mer show'r is

121

ROSALIE

Words and Music by
COLE PORTER

125

126

TOO DARN HOT

Words and Music by
COLE PORTER

132

TRUE LOVE

Words and Music by
COLE PORTER

WELL, DID YOU EVAH?

Words and Music by
COLE PORTER

WHAT IS THIS THING CALLED LOVE?

Words and Music by
COLE PORTER

WUNDERBAR

(From "KISS ME KATE")

Words and Music by
COLE PORTER

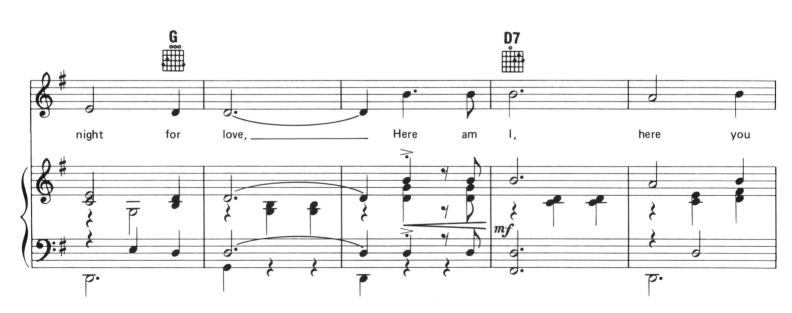

148

YOU DO SOMETHING TO ME

Words and Music by
COLE PORTER

153

YOU'D BE SO NICE TO COME HOME TO

(From "SOMETHING TO SHOUT ABOUT")

Words and Music by
COLE PORTER

157

YOU'RE THE TOP

Words and Music by
COLE PORTER

160